1000 MORE WORDS

Penguin
Random
House

Written by Gill Budgell
Senior Editor Dawn Sirett
Senior Designer Rachael Parfitt Hunt
Designers Kanika Kalra, Mansi Dwivedi, Rhys Thomas, Sif Nørskov
US Editor Jane Perlmutter
US Senior Editor Shannon Beatty
Additional editorial work Robin Moul
Additional illustrations Rhys Thomas, Mohd Zishan
DTP Designers Dheeraj Singh, Syed Md Farhan
Picture Researcher Rituraj Singh
Jacket Designer Sif Nørskov
Jacket Coordinator Elin Woosnam
Production Editor Becky Fallowfield
Production Controller John Casey
Managing Editor Penny Smith
Delhi Creative Head Malavika Talukder
Art Director Mabel Chan
Publisher Francesca Young
Publishing Director Sarah Larter

First American Edition, 2024
Published in the United States by DK Publishing,
a division of Penguin Random House LLC
1745 Broadway, 20th Floor, New York, NY 10019

A catalog record for this book
is available from the Library of Congress.
ISBN: 978–0–7440–9828–0

DK books are available at special discounts when purchased in bulk
for sales promotions, premiums, fund-raising, or educational use.
For details, contact: DK Publishing Special Markets,
1745 Broadway, 20th Floor, New York, NY 10019
SpecialSales@dk.com

Printed and bound in China

www.dk.com

MIX
Paper | Supporting
responsible forestry
FSC™ C018179

This book was made with Forest
Stewardship Council™ certified
paper—one small step in DK's
commitment to a sustainable future.
Learn more at
www.dk.com/uk/information/sustainability

1000 MORE WORDS

Gill Budgell

A note for parents and caregivers about language for learning

This book focuses on more of the vocabulary young children need for their learning whether in school or in their everyday lives.

As children learn, they need to read, write, and spell words that relate to a variety of topics and subjects. They need to be able to listen and speak with confidence too.

1000 More Words features vocabulary that will help children learn about literacy skills, mathematics, science, the arts, PE, and sports, as well as some more challenging vocabulary about geography and history. There are also words about technology, since increasingly the language of technology is embedded in every aspect of our learning. We talk about digital communication, digital devices, as well as ways to create and present information in a more data-led world.

A broad vocabulary can help children access their education more easily with a sense of curiosity and engagement. It enables them to name, describe, explain, and sort their learning into categories, as well as to see overlaps between different areas of learning.

Spending time with children to talk about the words and pictures representing different areas of learning within this book will ensure that children consolidate what they know and extend their knowledge and understanding. This book is a great place to begin sharing words and enjoying discussions with your child, but remember to continue the conversations in your day-to-day life too.

Gill Budgell
Early years and primary language consultant, trainer, and author

Contents

Let's communicate

When we communicate we share information, stories, feelings, or ideas. There are many ways to do this, including speaking, signing, writing, or dancing. Here are words we use for these things.

Communication

speak   discuss   listen

sign

present   ask

join in

dance

act

paint

Learning to read

letters

Braille

words
picture
This is my friend.
sentence
book

Learning to write

writing guidelines

copying and tracing

hello (English) left to right

مرحبا ("hello" in Arabic) right to left

新年快乐 top to bottom

("Happy New Year" in Chinese)

Languages are written left to right, right to left, or sometimes top to bottom.

Feelings

amazed

satisfied

Try making the faces for these feelings.

brave

upset

puzzled

shy

excited

frustrated

7

Reading and writing

Why do we read and write? Reading helps us learn and gives us pleasure. Writing helps us communicate and record our communications. Here are words we use when we read and write.

Different types of reading

independent   paired   shared   guided

What books do you like to read?

Fiction

stories

fantasy

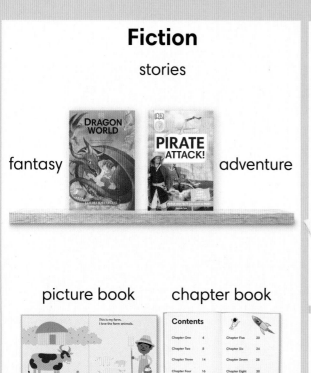

adventure

picture book   chapter book

Nonfiction

information

dictionary

report

newspaper   instructions

Reading everywhere!

OPEN

sign   label

JAM

board game

How to play

instructions

Braille is used by people who are blind or have low vision.

raised dots that you feel

Let's write!

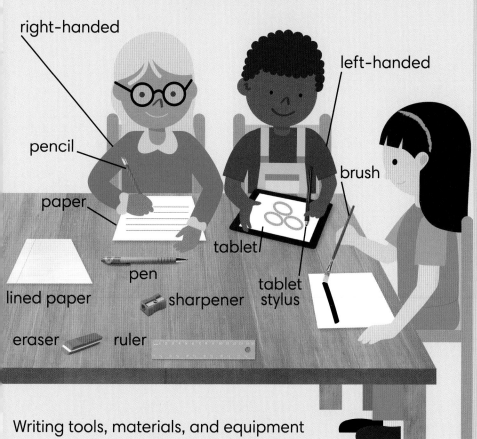

right-handed

pencil

paper

lined paper

eraser   ruler

pen

sharpener

tablet

left-handed

brush

tablet stylus

Writing tools, materials, and equipment

Preparing to write

thinking

ideas

Reasons to write

Books to read

list

Happy   birthday!

card

Remember to brush your teeth!

note

Please come to my party.

invitation

Dear friend,

letter

Adding up

Add up the numbers on the sails.
Write the total on the boats.

homework

Kitten gets stuck!

planning

Languages of the world

The languages we speak are part of who we are. Let's find out how to write and pronounce "hello" in ten of the most widely spoken languages in the world.

Chinese

你好

Chinese script

Say "nee-how."

Russian

привет

Cyrillic script

Say "pri-vyet."

Japanese

こんにちは

hiragana script

Say "kon-nee-chee-wah."

Arabic

مرحبا

Arabic abjad script

Say "mar-haba."

Hindi

नमस्ते

Devanagari script

Say "nuh-must-ay."

Bengali

হ্যালো

Bengali script

Say "hel-o."

Korean

안녕하세요

Hangul script

Say "ann-yong-ha-sey-oh."

English

Hello

Latin script

Say "hel-low."

Spanish

Hola

Latin script

Say "oh-la."

Portuguese — accent

Olá

Latin script

Say "oh-la."

What languages do you speak?

"Hello" in sign language

Can you sign hello?

"Hello" in Braille
(a written code for languages)

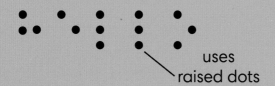

uses
raised dots

Whistling language
for long-distance
communication

Emojis

Computer code (programming language)

01000001   **01000010**   **01000011**

A   B   C

binary number system

Ancient languages

A   B   C   D   E

Sumerian
(from an area that is modern-day Iraq)

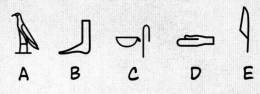

A   B   C   D   E

Egyptian hieroglyphs

Naming things

Words that name places, people, objects, animals, and ideas are called nouns.

At a hospital, we might use these nouns.

Places

reception

waiting room

consulting room

dispensary

emergency room

x-ray room

operating room

ward

People

patient

line

nurse

medical receptionist

doctor

paramedic

Objects

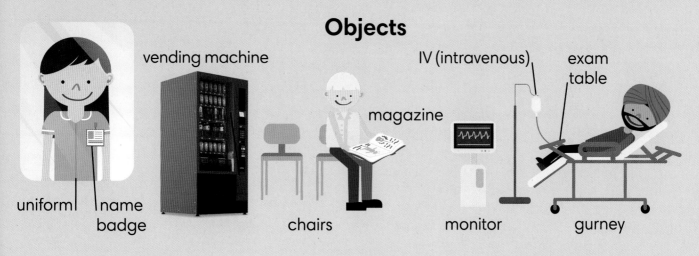

vending machine

magazine

IV (intravenous)

exam table

uniform | name badge

chairs

monitor

gurney

Ideas

healthy eating

thought

strength

success

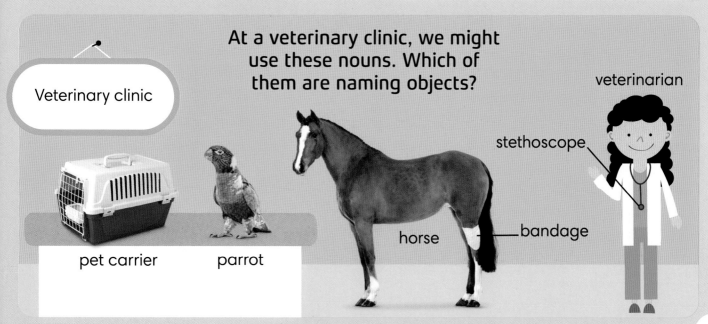

Veterinary clinic

At a veterinary clinic, we might use these nouns. Which of them are naming objects?

veterinarian

stethoscope

horse

bandage

pet carrier

parrot

Describing things

Words that describe people, places, objects, animals, and ideas are called adjectives. Choose an adjective that describes you!

talented

friendly

chatty

People

tall

skillful

young

sleepy

ravenous

Feelings

joyful

dizzy

comfortable

Size and volume

supersized

enormous

tiny

overflowing

yummy

juicy

chilled

fruity

steady

quickly

Food

sugary

fresh

spicy

chocolatey

Movement

speedy

smelly

sparkling

scorching

beige

vibrant

Color

vivid

15

What's going on?

Some words describe what people or things are doing, or what people are thinking or feeling. These words are called verbs.

Which of these things would you like to do?

prepare

reach

Stretch!

frown

What would you like?

ask

decide

dislike

lick

forget

Stop!

notice

skip

pull

block

kick

sniff

17

Adding detail

We can add detail to verbs by using words that say how, when, where, how often, and how much a thing happens. These words are called adverbs.

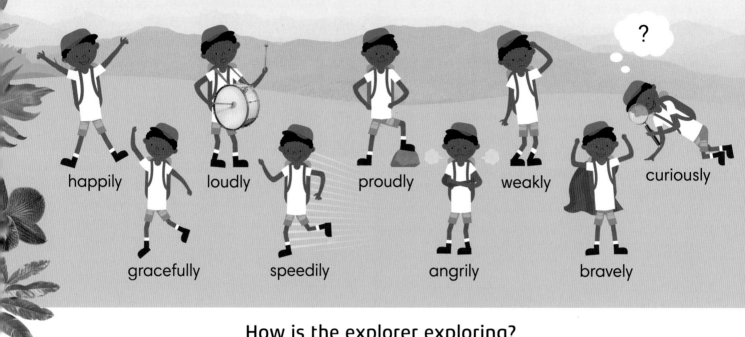

happily   loudly   proudly   weakly   curiously

gracefully   speedily   angrily   bravely

How is the explorer exploring?

today   soon   now   tomorrow

When should the explorer go exploring?

Where is the beetle climbing? Where is the beetle positioned?

How often and how much do the birds sing?

How often do the frogs eat?

All about numbers

Here are words that help us play counting games and learn about numbers.

Playing with numbers

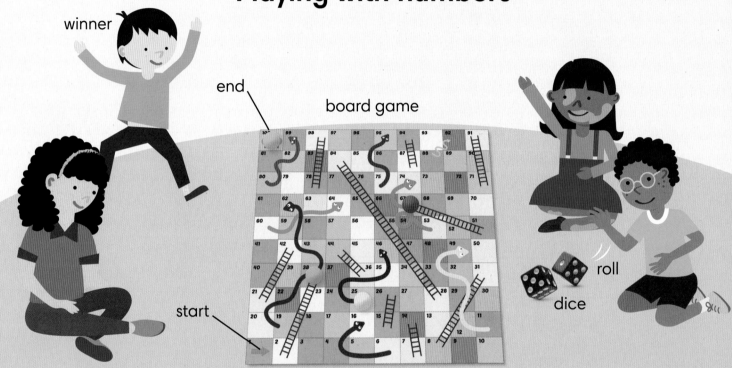

winner

end

board game

start

roll

dice

Types of numbers

2, 4, 6, 8, 10
even numbers

1, 3, 5, 7, 9
odd numbers

13, 14, 15, 16, 17, 18, 19
teen numbers

Place value

3
3 ones

30
3 tens

300
3 hundreds

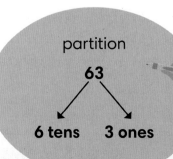

partition

63

6 tens   **3 ones**

Counting

5, 10, 15, 20, 25
in fives

10, 20, 30, 40, 50
in tens

Ordinals

sixth   fifth   fourth   third   second   first

What are the missing numbers?

_____ ← 20
before

11 _____ 13
between

17 → _____
after

Order these numbers from lowest to highest.

27   25   26

Number bonds

part   part   part   part   part   part

2   4   6   0   5   1

6   6   6
whole   whole   whole

Addition

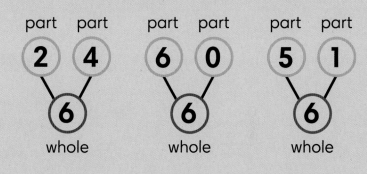

3   2   5

Subtraction

3   2   1

Shapes and space

Let's learn some shape names and some words about position and direction.

2D shape

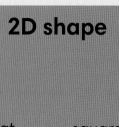

flat   square

4 corners

4 sides

Lines of symmetry for a square

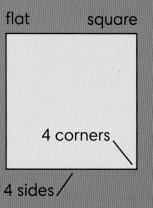

1   2

3

4

4 symmetry lines

3D shapes

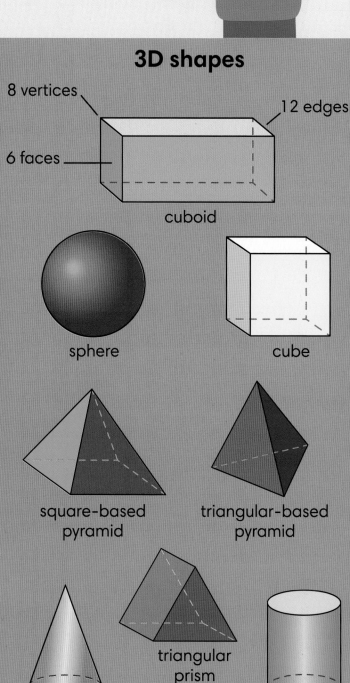

8 vertices

12 edges

6 faces

cuboid

sphere

cube

square-based pyramid

triangular-based pyramid

cone

triangular prism

cylinder

Polygons (2D shapes with 3 or more straight sides)

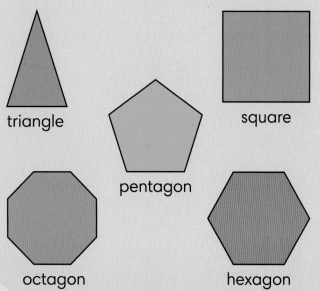

triangle

pentagon

square

octagon

hexagon

Can you see any of these shapes near you?

22

Position and direction

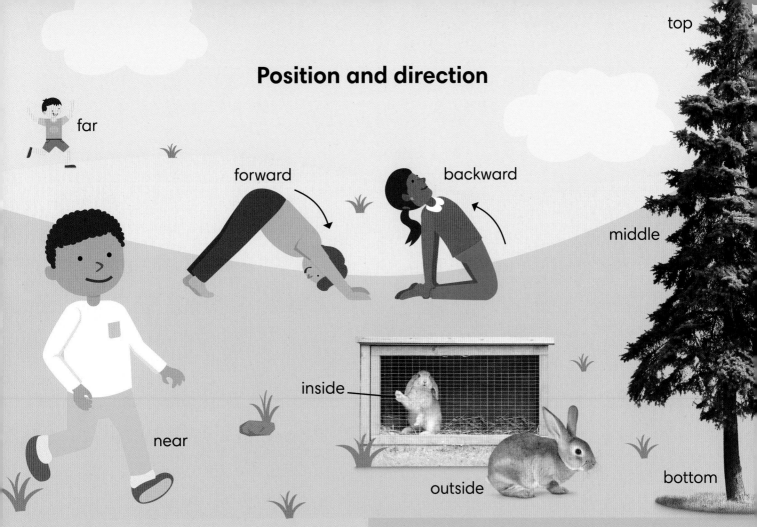

top

far

forward

backward

middle

inside

near

outside

bottom

Rotations

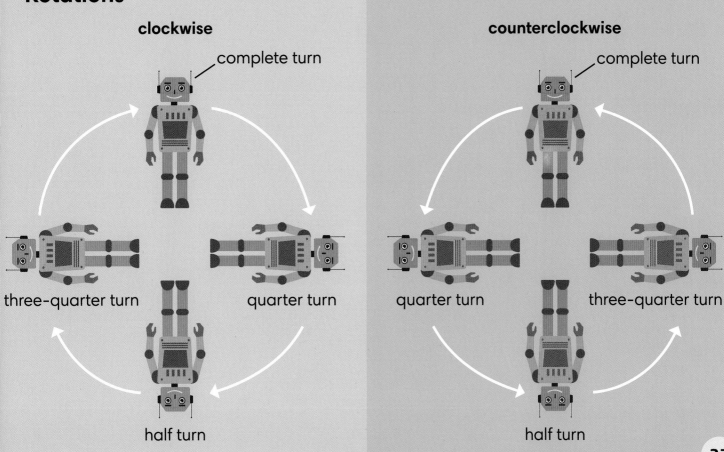

clockwise

complete turn

three-quarter turn

quarter turn

half turn

counterclockwise

complete turn

quarter turn

three-quarter turn

half turn

Talking about science

Here are some words we use when we are working together in science.

Can you think of some more equipment that you might use in a science lesson?

Let's be scientists

notice

observe

sort

classify

ask questions

Some things we might use

water food coloring measuring spoons microscope

scale stopwatch funnel magnet

containers safety goggles

compare contrast gather data

Let's experiment

prepare

fill

add

stir

help

pour

make

Adding salt to soda

describe

The drink fizzes and rises up!

note sounds and smells

record results

Describing materials

Let's learn some words to help us describe everyday materials.

Natural materials

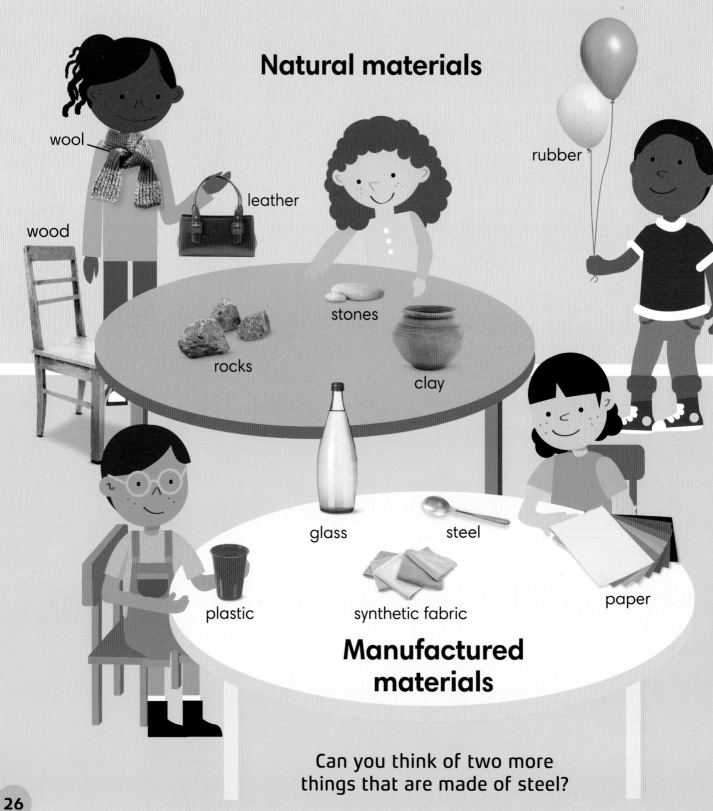

wool

wood

leather

stones

rocks

clay

rubber

glass

steel

plastic

synthetic fabric

paper

Manufactured materials

Can you think of two more things that are made of steel?

Opposites

transparent   opaque

shiny   dull

hard   soft

stretchy   rigid

waterproof   not waterproof

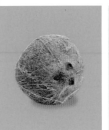 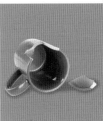

tough   brittle

absorbent   not absorbent

heavy   light

fluffy   spiky

rough   bumpy   smooth

 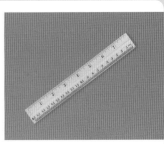

bendable   flexible   stiff

All about art

Here are words about art and the names of some tools we use to make different kinds of art. Think of a picture you would like to create. What tool would you use to create it?

Mark making

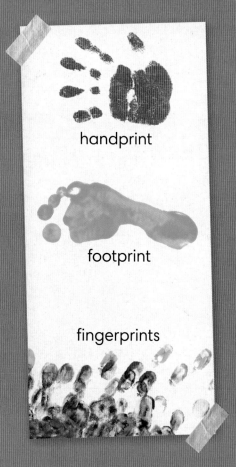

handprint

footprint

fingerprints

quill

pens

marker

pencils

ink

crayons

charcoal

chalk

wooden stamp

paints

Making things

sculpture

painting

collage

architecture

pottery

Digital art

photography

camera

zoom lens

close-up

long shot

animation

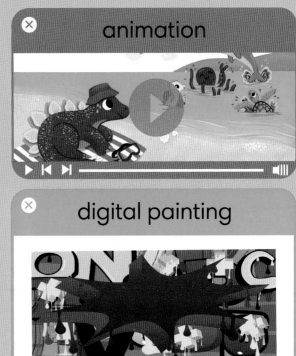

digital painting

Colors

primary colors

mixing colors

Tones

tint

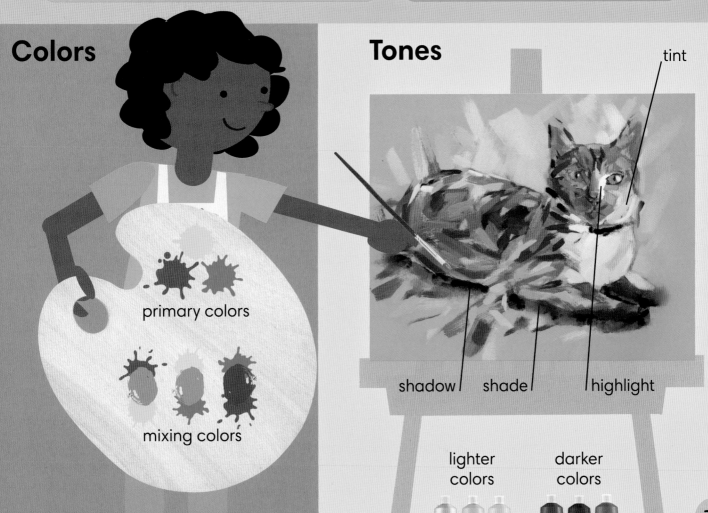

shadow

shade

highlight

lighter colors

darker colors

Lines and patterns

These words help us to describe patterns and designs. What patterns do you like?

If you were decorating a T-shirt with lines, which of the lines below would you choose?

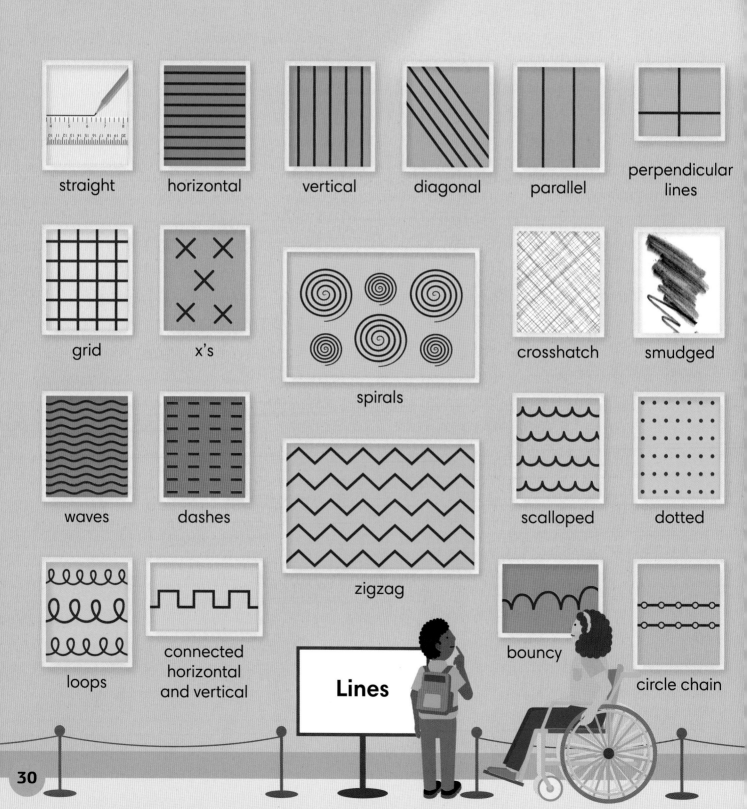

straight

horizontal

vertical

diagonal

parallel

perpendicular lines

grid

x's

spirals

crosshatch

smudged

waves

dashes

zigzag

scalloped

dotted

loops

connected horizontal and vertical

Lines

bouncy

circle chain

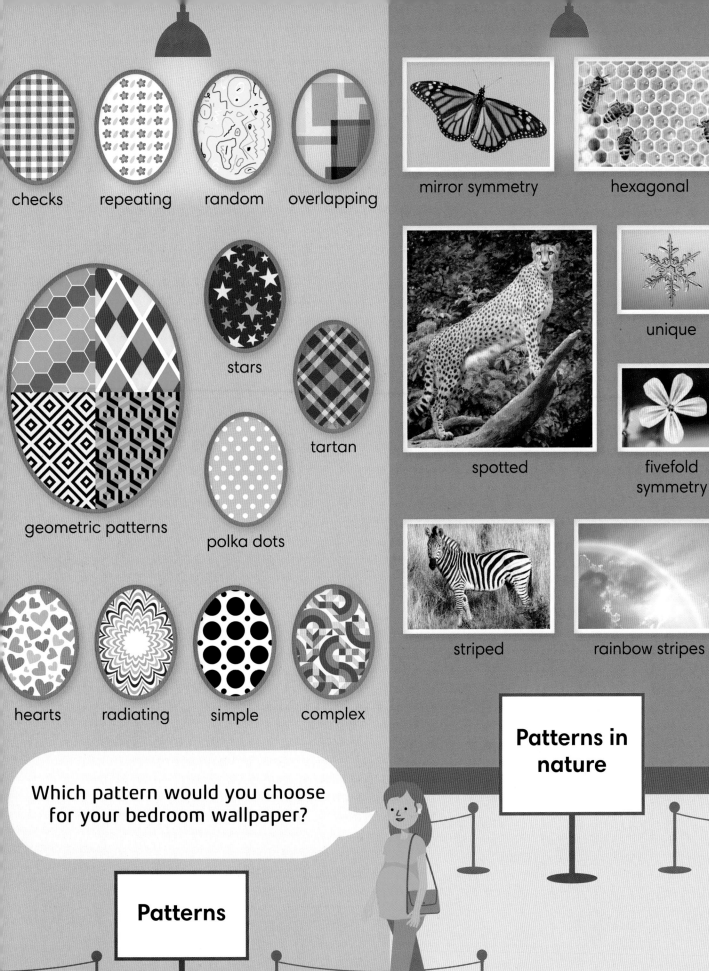

checks

repeating

random

overlapping

mirror symmetry

hexagonal

geometric patterns

stars

tartan

polka dots

unique

spotted

fivefold symmetry

hearts

radiating

simple

complex

striped

rainbow stripes

Patterns in nature

Which pattern would you choose for your bedroom wallpaper?

Patterns

Designing and making

Here are words we use when we design and make things, and words for tools and machines. What would you like to make?

Designing

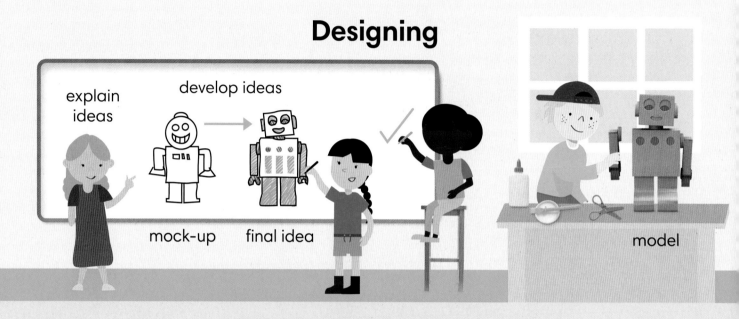

explain ideas

develop ideas

mock-up

final idea

model

Making

cutting

constructing

shaping

weaving

Joining

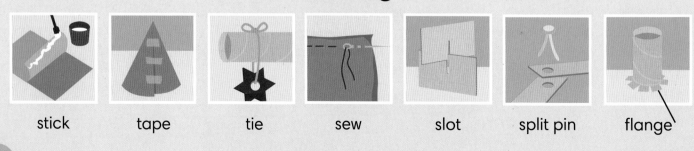

stick

tape

tie

sew

slot

split pin

flange

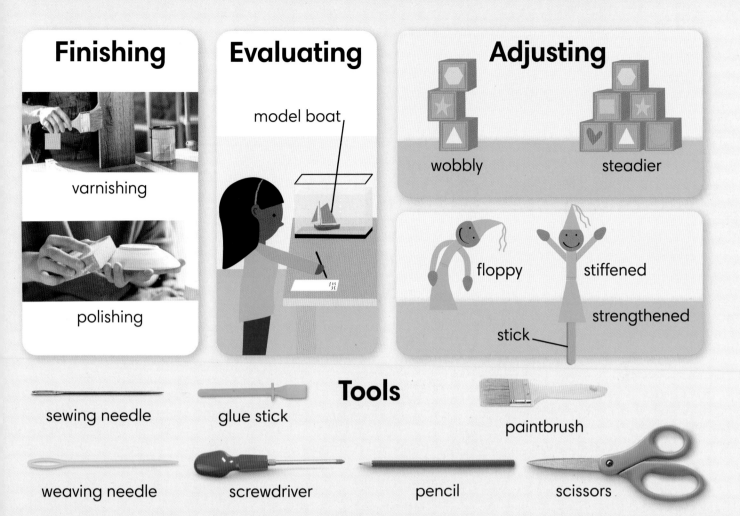

Finishing

varnishing

polishing

Evaluating

model boat

Adjusting

wobbly　　steadier

floppy　　stiffened

strengthened

stick

Tools

sewing needle

glue stick

paintbrush

weaving needle

screwdriver

pencil

scissors

Simple machines and technology

lever

load

effort

pulley

ladder

fulcrum

screw

wheels

axle

ramp

chassis (body)

Talking about cooking

These words name cooking equipment and help us talk about activities we do in the kitchen.

What equipment might you use when making a cake?

Preparing to cook

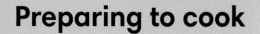

put on an apron

clean and dry surfaces

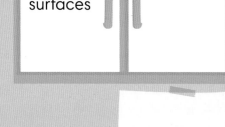
cleaning cloths

Always ask an adult to help you when cooking and when using knives.

wash your hands

Kitchen utensils

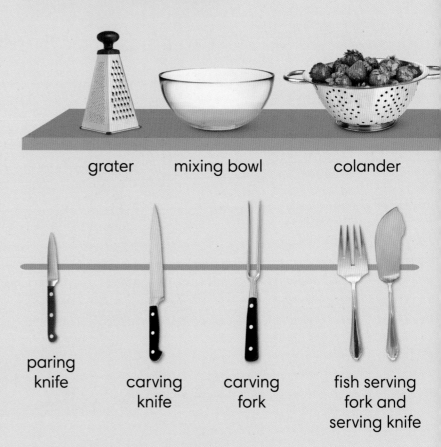

grater   mixing bowl   colander

paring knife

carving knife

carving fork

fish serving fork and serving knife

Cooking

make cakes

cakes in a baking pan

wok

immersion blender

tongs

spatula

ladle

whisk

wooden spoon

pitcher

funnel

rolling pin

cutting board

cookie cutter

pot

pastry brush

ice-cream scoop

strainer

can opener

frying pan

Cleaning up

do the dishes

dish soap

spray cleaner

load the dishwasher

dish sponge

wipe surfaces

Different foods

Here are words for some foods and the main food groups. The study of food and how it works in our bodies is called "nutrition." What's important is enjoying food and eating healthily.

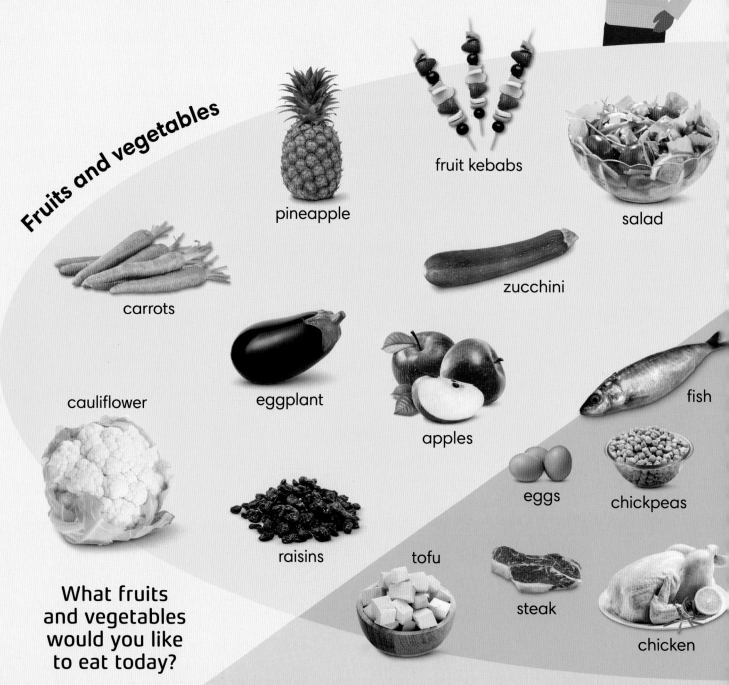

Fruits and vegetables

pineapple

fruit kebabs

salad

carrots

zucchini

cauliflower

eggplant

apples

fish

eggs

chickpeas

raisins

tofu

steak

chicken

What fruits and vegetables would you like to eat today?

Proteins

Where is your food from?

bread → wheat

ginger → underground stem of the ginger plant

blueberries → blueberry plant

chocolate → seeds of the cacao tree

fruit smoothie

cookies

oats

pasta

pitas

noodles

baguette

bran flakes

potatoes

Starchy carbohydrates

soy milk

nuts

coconut yogurt

butter

olive oil

rice

kidney beans

cheese

milk

Oils

Dairy and dairy alternatives

Know your world

Some nouns help us to name different places on Earth, including lands and oceans. We also use nouns for the directions on a compass.

Rocky Mountains

Compass

North
Northwest   Northeast
West   East
Southwest   Southeast
South

North America

Pacific Ocean

Atlantic Ocean

Viewing our world

Atlas
atlas

globe

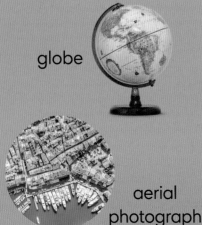
aerial photograph

Amazon rainforest

equator

South America

Point to the part of the world you live in.

Antarctic desert

cold desert

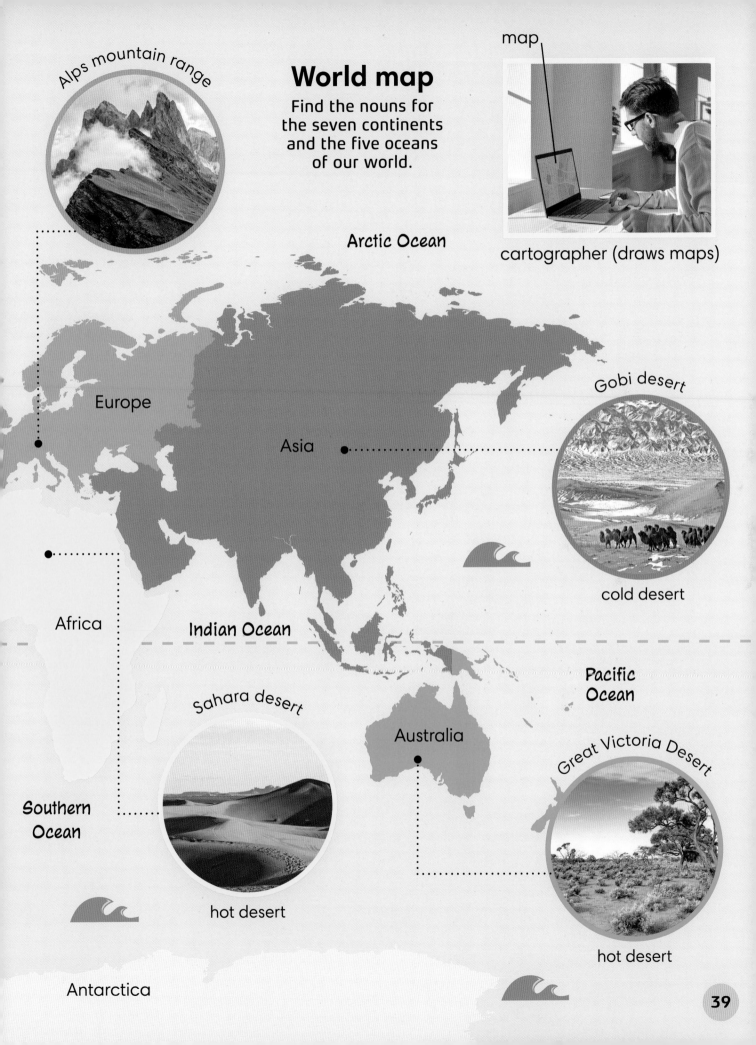

Alps mountain range

World map
Find the nouns for
the seven continents
and the five oceans
of our world.

map

cartographer (draws maps)

Arctic Ocean

Europe

Asia

Gobi desert

cold desert

Africa

Indian Ocean

Pacific
Ocean

Sahara desert

Australia

Great Victoria Desert

Southern
Ocean

hot desert

hot desert

Antarctica

Natural landscapes and seascapes

These words name natural areas of the land and the ocean in our world. Some of these places are protected because they are so spectacular and unique.

Which of the places in these pictures would you like to visit?

Land

coast

peninsula

mountain range

dry canyon

mound

cave

lowlands

highlands

Water

sea

bay

harbor

lagoon

inlet

atoll

lake

river

stream

river gorge

waterfall

glacier

Some plant environments

forest   woodland

rainforest

savanna

prairie

tundra

Protected places

national park   wilderness area

nature reserve

natural monument

protected seascape

World Heritage sites

Created landscapes

Here are words for places, buildings, and other things that are created in landscapes by humans. Are you sitting in a building? What is it called?

Where we live and work

village

town

city

farm

house

cottage

apartment building

store

school

office

factory

Services

port

pier

lighthouse

dam

reservoir

oil rig

transmission towers

wind farm

bicycle lane

direction signs

overpass

bridge

railroad bridge

drain

sewer

Fun places to visit

park

adventure park

water park

recreation center

petting zoo

museum

statue

castle ruins

ancient wall

prehistoric monument

Long, long ago

We name large groups of people from long ago "ancient civilizations." They existed thousands of years ago. Here are some ancient civilizations. Objects from the past help us learn about them.

Find some words that mean ruler or monarch.

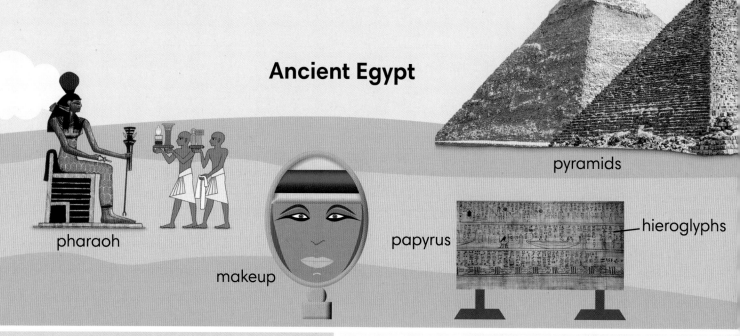

Ancient Egypt

pyramids

pharaoh

makeup

papyrus

hieroglyphs

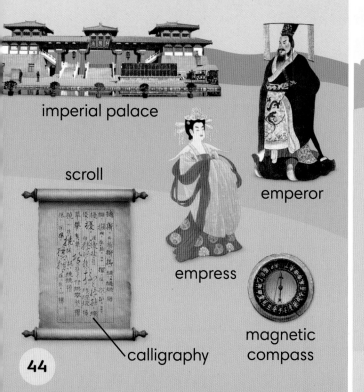

Ancient China

imperial palace

scroll

emperor

empress

calligraphy

magnetic compass

44

Mesoamerica

temple

Mayans

Mayan calendar system

Mayan headdress

lord

lady

Ancient Rome

aqueduct

emperor

empress

Romans

gladiator

Roman road

The Ghana Empire

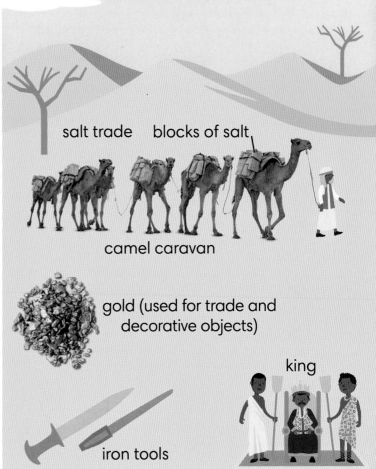

salt trade   blocks of salt

camel caravan

gold (used for trade and decorative objects)

king

iron tools

Ancient Greece

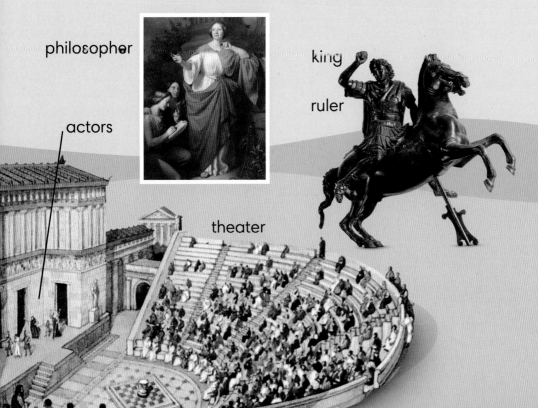

philosopher

king

ruler

actors

theater

ancient Olympic Games

discus throwing

chariot racing

Transportation over time

Like other things, transportation has changed over time.
Let's discover words for types of transportation through
the ages. Which of these would you like to try?

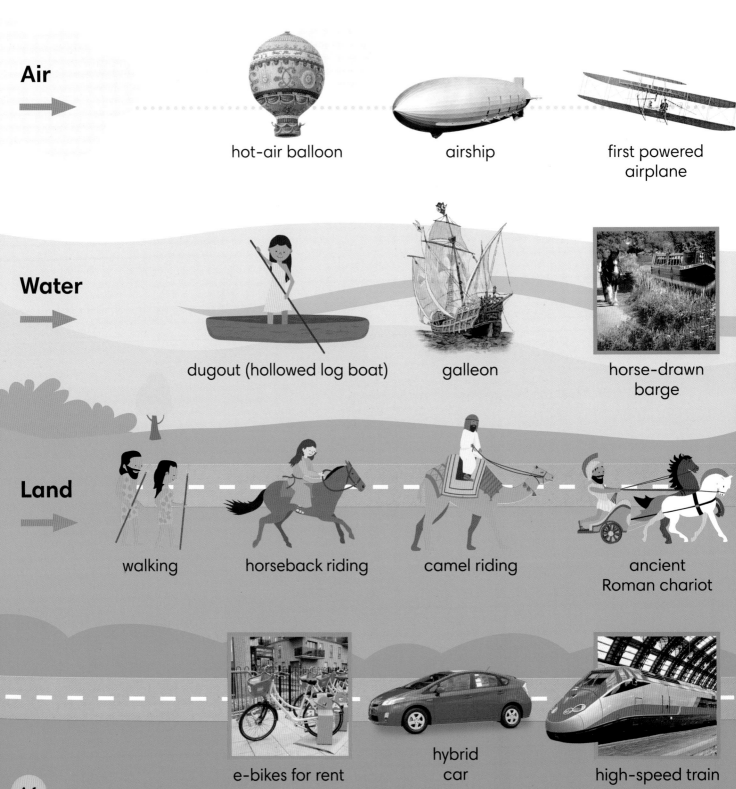

Air →

hot-air balloon

airship

first powered
airplane

Water →

dugout (hollowed log boat)

galleon

horse-drawn
barge

Land →

walking

horseback riding

camel riding

ancient
Roman chariot

e-bikes for rent

hybrid
car

high-speed train

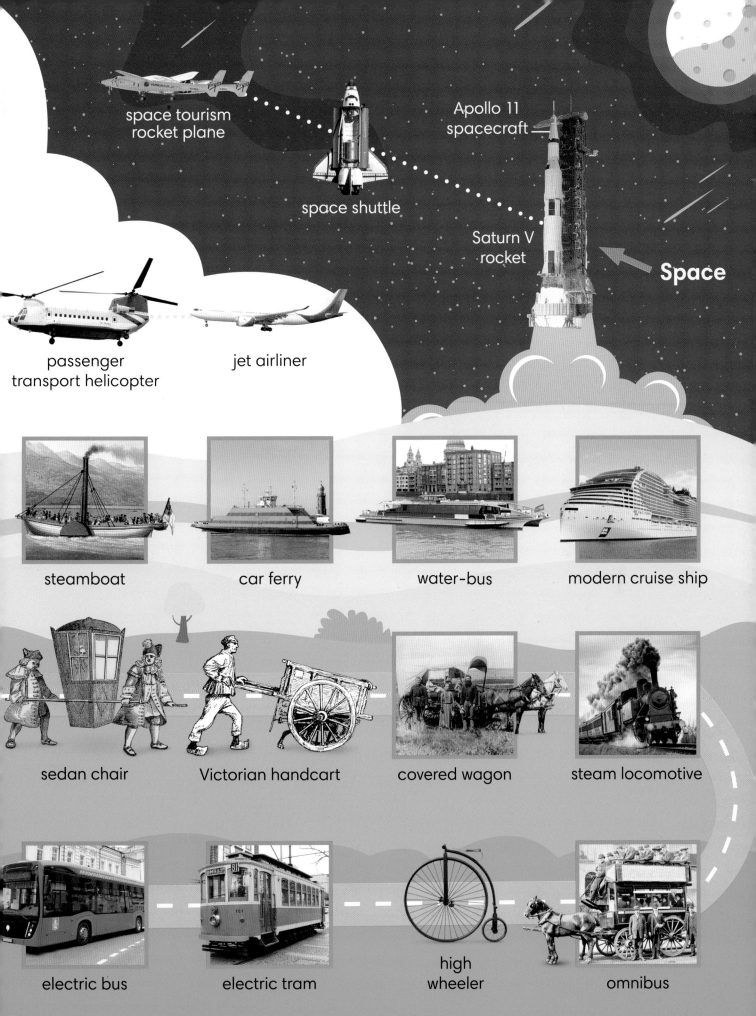

space tourism rocket plane

space shuttle

Apollo 11 spacecraft

Saturn V rocket

Space

passenger transport helicopter

jet airliner

steamboat

car ferry

water-bus

modern cruise ship

sedan chair

Victorian handcart

covered wagon

steam locomotive

electric bus

electric tram

high wheeler

omnibus

Digital communication

Here are words we use to talk about gadgets, computers, and sending information electronically. What digital devices have you used?

Digital devices

tablet

smartphone

digital camera

wireless earbuds

laptop

microphone

gaming headset

gaming console and gaming controller

television

screen, processor, memory, and hard drive

webcam

interactive whiteboard

mouse

desktop personal computer

keyboard

printer

We need to be very careful when using digital devices
so that we keep ourselves and our information safe.
Ask a trusted adult to help you with this.

Communication and computer symbols

log on

Username

Password

personal
information

privacy   security

satellite

Wi-Fi   document   compose   attachment

text   avatar

email

chatbot
(a computer
program that
replies to
messages)

Hey, how
are you?

I'm fine,
thanks!

chat   friends   sharing

apps

messaging

social media

video call

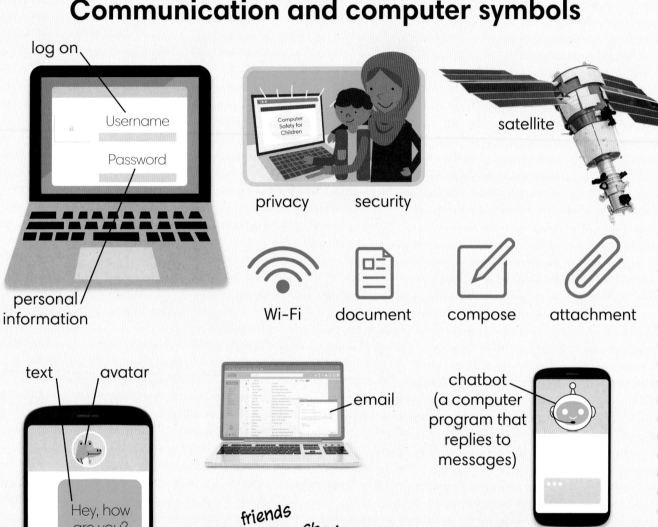

Creating and presenting

Let's look at words we use when we collect information, create something from information, and share information with others.

Finding information

Search

web browser

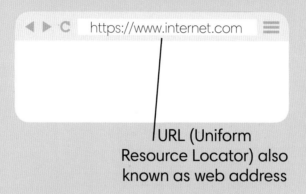

https://www.internet.com

URL (Uniform Resource Locator) also known as web address

reading and researching

asking questions

visiting a library

visiting a museum

going on a field trip

interviewing friends and family

collecting

finding pictures

Handling information

Leaf sizes

Big   Medium   Small

sort

Sorting fruit
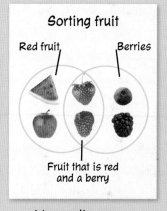

Red fruit   Berries

Fruit that is red
and a berry

Venn diagram

Which is the most popular pet?

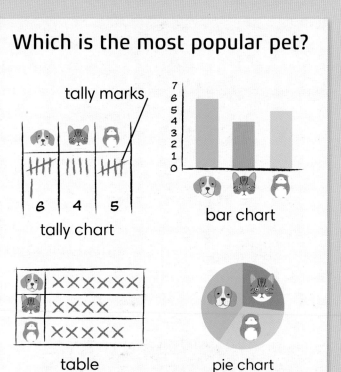

tally marks

tally chart

6   4   5

bar chart

table

pie chart

Plants questionnaire
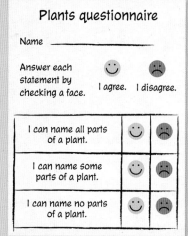

Name _____

Answer each
statement by
checking a face.   I agree.   I disagree.

I can name all parts of a plant.	☺	☹
I can name some parts of a plant.	☺	☹
I can name no parts of a plant.	☺	☹

questionnaire   survey

Growth of a sunflower
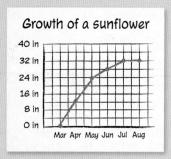

40 in
32 in
24 in
16 in
8 in
0 in
Mar Apr May Jun Jul Aug

graph

Creating

drawing pictures   making notes

filming

How to grow a sunflower

Presenting

How to grow a sunflower

poster

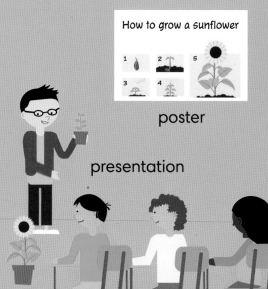

presentation

Slide 1

How to grow
a sunflower

A step-by-step guide

slideshow

vlog

blog

live stream

Technology innovations

The language we use for new toys and equipment is ever-changing. Some innovations are just for fun and games. Others help us with challenges in life.

Which of these things would you like to use?

Innovations that entertain us

talking electronic pet

virtual-reality headset

virtual-reality (VR) app
(makes you feel like you are in
a world created by a computer)

projector

touch-sensitive
plasma light

augmented-reality (AR) app
(puts 3D computer images
in the real world)

floor

voice-changer toy

wall

52

Innovations that help us (some entertain us too!)

e-book

e-reader

smartwatch

multitouch table

voice assistant

robotic prosthetic

gloves that change
sign language into speech

smart glasses that
read text out loud

e-scooters

e-microcar

camera
quadcopter drone

3D printer

adaptive gaming controller
(for gamers who have a disability)

green screen

USB microscope (for viewing
tiny images on a computer)

educational robot toy

portable water purifier

neck fan

robot waiter

Making music

We use these words when we talk and write about music. We can perform music in fun ways, solo or with others.

sound

Body percussion

snap

clap

stomp

pat

Performing music

solo

duet

choir

rock band

orchestra

rap group

Instruments

Percussion

mallets

xylophone

piano (percussion and strings)

tambourine

steel drums

drums

Strings

bow

violin   guitar

Do you play a musical instrument? If not, which instrument would you like to play?

Woodwind

clarinet

flute

Brass

French horn   trumpet

tuba

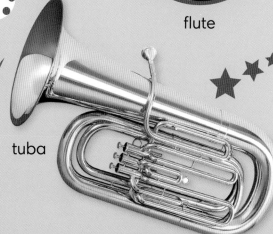

Reading music

musical notes

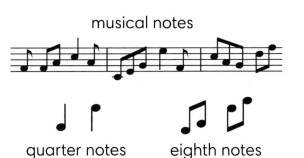

quarter notes

eighth notes

The speed of a piece of music (tempo)

adagio (slowly like a turtle's movement)

allegro (quickly like a cheetah's movement)

55

Playing sports

Here are words for some sports, some skills we use in sports, and some sports equipment. Which sports do you play or like to watch?

resilient

balancing

skateboarding

athletics

speed

table tennis

quick reflexes

swimming

floating

pickleball

teamwork

leaping

volleyball

wheelchair tennis

precision

soccer

accuracy

shin guard

attacking

defending

tactics

basketball

shooting

throwing

karate

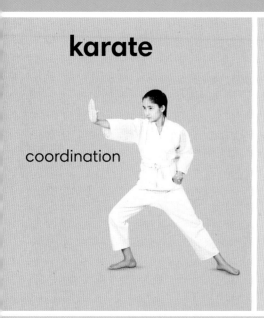

coordination

gymnastics

power

baseball

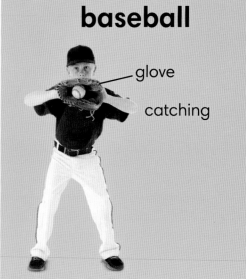

glove

catching

ice hockey

helmet

passing

endurance

mountain biking

57

Three super sports!

Let's learn words for different kinds of athletics, gymnastics, and swimming.

Which do you like best: running fast, swinging from bars in a playground, or splashing in a swimming pool?

Athletics

Track events

sprint

relay

long-distance running

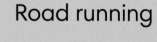
hurdles

steeplechase

Field events

high jump

pole vault

long jump

javelin

shot put

discus

hammer

Road running

marathon

Gymnastics

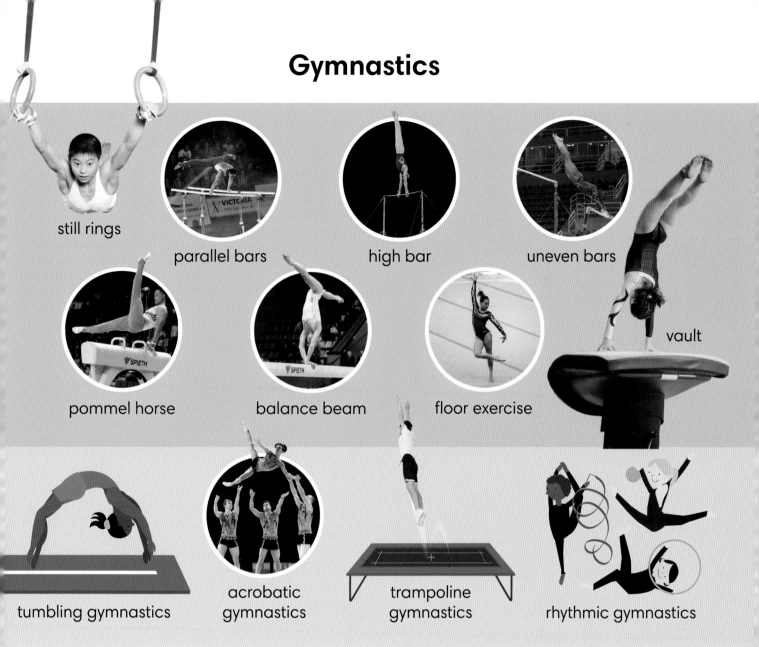

still rings

parallel bars

high bar

uneven bars

pommel horse

balance beam

floor exercise

vault

tumbling gymnastics

acrobatic gymnastics

trampoline gymnastics

rhythmic gymnastics

Swimming and diving

breaststroke

backstroke

butterfly

artistic swimming

diving

crawl

freestyle

Play and explore

We are learning even when we are playing. Let's discover words for play areas, learning areas, and fun play equipment.

Come and write!

writing area

painting area

Playing inside

reading fort

beanbag

dress-up area

sensory play

construction

playdough

You can play at any age!
How will you play when
you are grown up?

outdoor
stage

tree
swing

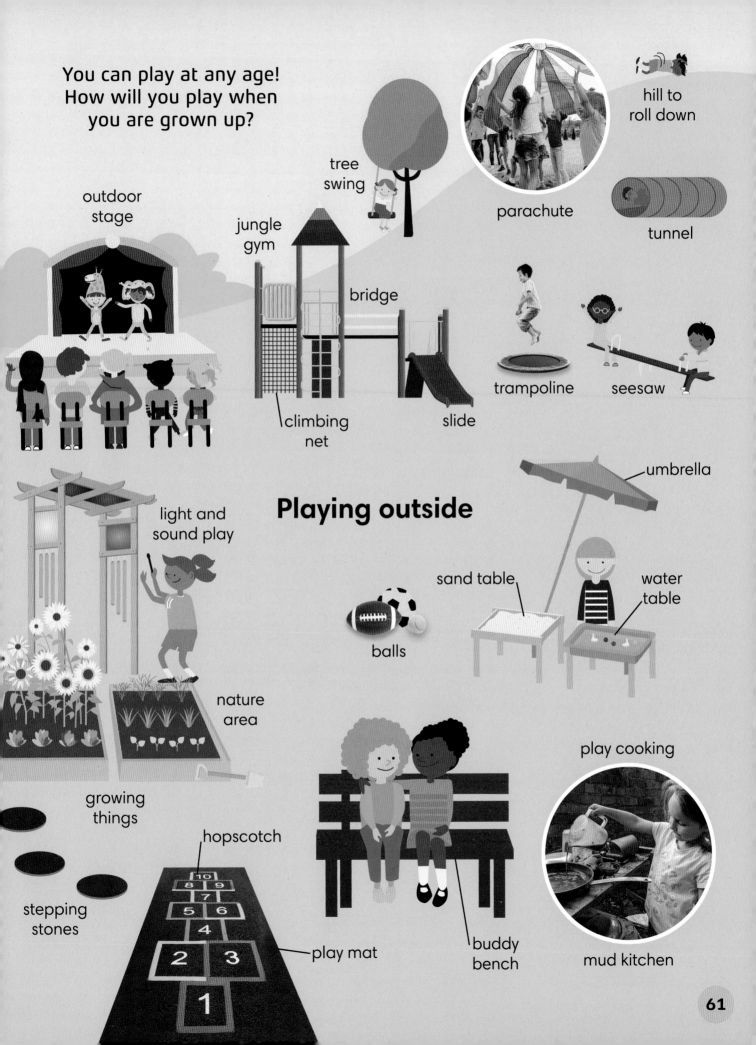

parachute

hill to
roll down

tunnel

jungle
gym

bridge

climbing
net

slide

trampoline

seesaw

light and
sound play

Playing outside

umbrella

sand table

water
table

balls

nature
area

play cooking

growing
things

hopscotch

10

8 9

7

5 6

4

stepping
stones

2 3

1

play mat

buddy
bench

mud kitchen

Learning everywhere!

Here are words we use to talk about school, clubs, and learning. We can learn anytime and anywhere, before, during, and after our school life.

At school

class lining up

taking attendance

lesson time

library time

break time

music

lunchtime

PE (physical education)

home time

school show

A learning time line

day care

preschool

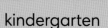

kindergarten

Clubs

art club

drama club

tennis club

sailing club

cooking club

Choose a club you'd like to join.

dance club

soccer club

Hola
language club

nature club

ski club

School trips and outings

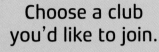
aquarium

natural history museum

art museum

nature park

castle

elementary school

high school

college

Acknowledgments

DK would like to thank: Dheeraj Arora for additional jacket design work; Geetam Biswas, Ridhima Sikka, Shubhdeep Kaur, Manpreet Kaur, and Samrajkumar for additional picture research work.

The publisher would like to thank the following for their kind permission to reproduce their photographs:
(Key: a=above; b=below/bottom; c=center; f=far; l=left; r=right; t=top)

1 Dreamstime.com: Isselee (cb); Johnfoto (br). 2 Dreamstime.com: Maglara (bl). 3 123RF.com: lucyfry (cb); Rose-Marie Henriksson / rosemhenri (tl). Dreamstime.com: Photoeuphoria (clb). 6 Alamy Stock Photo: H. Mark Weidman Photography (bc); Myrleen Pearson (cla). Depositphotos Inc: belchonock (bl). Dreamstime.com: Monkey Business Images (br); Wavebreakmedia Ltd (cra); Yuri Arcurs (crb). Getty Images / iStock: E+ / sturti (clb). 7 123RF.com: microstockasia (c); nk2549 (cb/Brave). Dreamstime.com: Bellevue (bc/Door); Roman Milert (tr); Thammasak Chuenchom (cl); Chung Jin Mac (tr); Siew Mei Wong (cra); Vitaly Titov (crb); Yevgen Rychko (br). Getty Images / iStock: E+ / SDI Productions (cb); Olga Ignatova (cb); E+ / davidf (bl); Mr_Khan (bc); evgenyatamanenko (bc/Excited). 8 Depositphotos Inc: mstockagency (crb/Sign). Dreamstime.com: Elisabeth Burrell (cb/Dictionary); Krischam (clb/x2); Hryhorii Turik (cb). Getty Images / iStock: lleerogers (crb/Jar). Getty Images: PhotoAlto Agency RF Collections / Frederic Cirou (br). Shutterstock.com: Mister_X (crb). 9 123RF.com: chrupka (bc). Depositphotos Inc: luminastock (clb/Notepad). Dreamstime.com: Atman (cb/Eraser); Christophe Testi (cla); Boggy (ca/Brush); Sergii Kolesnyk (cla/Paper); Nao5970 (ca); Jose Manuel Gelpi Diaz (cla/Sharpner); Pearljamfan75 (cla/Pen); Alexandr Kornienko (cla/Table); Pictac (ca/Ruler); Thinglass (crb); Ruth Black (bl). Shutterstock.com: pikcha (ca/Tablet). 10 Dreamstime.com: Wirestock (cb/Hangul script). Shutterstock.com: KHARANI (Script). 11 Alamy Stock Photo: F1online digitale Bildagentur GmbH / f1 online (tr/mountain); Tony French (tr, tr/Man). Getty Images / iStock: hakule (cb); petekarici (tl, tc). Shutterstock.com: Mona Ahmed (br). 13 Dreamstime.com: Isselee (cb, bc). Shutterstock.com: arsa35 (cla). 14 Dreamstime.com: Torsakarin (bl/Carpet). Getty Images / iStock: Salmon Negro (tr). 15 123RF.com: Rose-Marie Henriksson / rosemhenri (br). Dreamstime.com: Hafiza Samsuddin (tl); Guido Vrola (bl/coke); Torsakarin (cr/Carpet); Pantila Terada (crb); Anke Van Wyk (bl/Steak). Getty Images / iStock: clubfoto (cla/Fruit); E+ / LauriPatterson (cla). 16 123RF.com: Oksana Tkachuk (cb/Flower). Dorling Kindersley: Stephen Oliver (cr). Dreamstime.com: Grafner (r/2xIce cream); Pytyczech (bl); Mikhail Kokhanchikov (bc). 17 123RF.com: Ekaterina Pereverzeva (r/2xMusic notes). Dreamstime.com: Milic Djurovic (ca/Slide); Eastmanphoto (cra/Squirrel); Svetlana Foote (tr/Bird). Getty Images / iStock: Antagain (bl). 18 123RF.com: gongzstudio (ca/Speed line). Dreamstime.com: Alexstar (cra/Magnifying); Saravn (cl/br); Boris Medvedev (cla/Drum); Taweesak Sriwannawit (bl). Getty Images / iStock: lightphoto (Background). 19 123RF.com: Aliaksei Hintau / viselchak (crb/Dragonfly); Eric Isselee (cla). Dorling Kindersley: Andy and Gill Swash (clb). Dreamstime.com: Michael Chatt (bc/Meadowlark); Mikelane45 (clb/Wren); Zhbampton (ca/10xBeetle); Prapass Wannapinij / Prapass (cra); Geza Farkas (cb); Isselee (crb); Mark Turner (crb/Meganeura); Sean Pavone (br/2xPond). Getty Images / iStock: lightphoto (bl/4xBackground). Shutterstock.com: Milano M (cb/Calendar); Aleksandr Pobedimskiy (cra/Sandstone, ca/2xSandstone). 20 Dreamstime.com: BigApple orathai hanthong (b); Mister_X (c); Mega Pixel (cr/Dice). 21 123RF.com: tinna2727 (cla). Dreamstime.com: Juan Hernandez Carmona (br/Buttons); Ennjee (tr/Poles); Studioloco (cra). Getty Images: Moment / Sergey Mironov (cra/Track). Getty Images / iStock: shapecharge (ca). Shutterstock.com: FamVeld (tl). 23 Alamy Stock Photo: Geoff du Feu (cra/Cage). Dreamstime.com: Roman Milert (tr). 24 Depositphotos Inc: stockimagefactory.com (clb). Dreamstime.com: Aprescindere (crb); Pavel Kobysh (cla); Elena Schweitzer / Egal (cra); Chernetskaya (ca/Red bottle); Cloki (ca/Water); Palians (c/Stopwatch); Artiom Storojenco (cr); Madamlead (cb/Beaker); Anton Starikov (cb/Jug, cb/Bowl). Getty Images / iStock: E+ / pinstock (cb); urfinguss (cr). Shutterstock.com: Art_Photo (ca); Studio Romantic (ca). 25 Depositphotos Inc: assumption111 (br); stockimagefactory.com (cl/Boy). Dreamstime.com: Piotr Adamowicz (cb/Board); Tatyana Vychegzhanina (tl); Oleg Beloborodov (tl/Water); Yunkiphotoshot (tr/Girl); Vadim Zakharishchev (cl). Shutterstock.com: T.TATSU (cr). 26 Dreamstime.com: Andriy Dykun (cla); Odarka Rusanenko (cla/Scarf); Evgeny Karandaev (ca, cb/Bottle); PixMarket (cla); Anton Starikov (cl/Rocks, crb); Sirikornt (cl); Sarah2 (clb); Serg_velusceac (cb/Fabric). 27 123RF.com: belchonock (clb/Gloves); martyhaas (ca). Dreamstime.com: Vlad Ageshin (tl/Door); Nexus7 (tl); Fang Jia / Clarkfang (tc/Mirror); Audines (tc); Jiri Hera (tr); Sally Herbert (tr/Hat); Irina Tiumentseva (cla); Christophe Testi (cla/Pencil); Timages (ca/Boots); Elizabeth Cummings (cra); Luisangel70 (clb); Sharpshot (cb/Stone); George Tsartsianidis (cb); Anna Khomulo (crb); Alfio Scisetti (crb/Cactus); Ping20k (bl); LOFT39Studio (bl/Pebble); Mycolor (br/Ruler). Shutterstock.com: ChebanenkoAnn (br). 28 123RF.com: Dndavis (cla/Handprint); picsfive (6xTape). Dorling Kindersley: Dave King / Rotring UK Ltd (cra/Pencil). Dreamstime.com: MingWei Chan (cl); Hypermania37 (crb/Chalk); Alison Gibson (cla/Texture); Nui7711 (bl/Frame); Elena8888 (clb); Chotewang (bl); Dansopdedeel (bl/Painting); Tuja66 (bc); Steven Jones (br); Valpal (br/Pot). Getty Images / iStock: spinspinspin (cl/2xTexture). 29 Dreamstime.com: Sergey Kolesnikov (cla/Close up, cra); Linusy (clb/Splashes). Getty Images / iStock: ChamilleWhite (bl); Silmen (br/Easels); Bob Vector (cra); tovovan (br). Getty Images: Maria Swrd (cla/2xLandscape). 30 Dreamstime.com: Andrey Golubtsov (cla); Hibrida13 (cr/crosshatch); Katrintimoff (cr). 31 Dreamstime.com: Svitlana Borokh (cla/Diamond); Ihor Patsay (cla/Hexagon); Cienpies Design / Illustrations (cla/3d hexagon); Samolevsky (cla); arko Savic (tl); Costasz (tc); Pimmimemom (tr/Butterfly); Aleksandr Rybalko (tr); Doozydo (ca/Stars); Witchera (ca); Serkorkin (cb); Rebius (cra/Cheetah); Lukas Jonaitis (cra); Maria Castellanos (cra/Flower); Vectorsoul (clb); Gabriel Robledo (crb/Zebra). Getty Images / iStock: DigitalVision Vectors / ulimi (clb/Hearts). Shutterstock.com: PongMoji (cra). 32 Dorling Kindersley: Dave King / Jemma Westing (cra). Dreamstime.com: Ansis (cb); Lightfieldsstudiosprod (clb/Cutting); Mariia Symchych Navrotska (clb); Jinaritt Thongruay (crb/Weaving). Getty Images / iStock: UroshPetrovic (cra/Robot). Shutterstock.com: Hilch (cla). 33 123RF.com: Milic Djurovic (crb/Ladder). Dreamstime.com: Jaroslaw Grudzinski / jarek78 (clb/Screw); Victor Savushkin (cla/Needle); Dmitry Marchenko (cla); Alfio Scisetti (cra). Shutterstock.com: 3Dalia (clb); Hayran1 (cl); Olezzo (tl). 34 Dreamstime.com: Luisa Vallon Fumi (cr); Melica (ca); Anton Starikov (ca/Bowl); Wolna (cra); Bohuslav Jelen (c/x2). Getty Images / iStock: Garrett Aitken (clb); Baloncici (clb/Green towel). 35 123RF.com: lucyfry (ca/Star). Dreamstime.com: Blackslide (tl/Wok); VectorHome (tl); Gavran333 (tc/Tongs, ca/Board); Eric Simard (tc); Maglara (ca); Viacheslav Krisanov (ca); Nikolai Sorokin (cra); Desiga (cl); Littleman (cb); Thomas Gowanlock (cr); Dio5050 (br). 36 Dreamstime.com: Andersastphoto (clb/Cauliflower); Fortyforks (cra/Salad); Hyrman (cl); Jaroslaw Grudzinski (c); Rimglow (cb); Kkovaleva (cb/Apples); Edward Westmacott (crb/Fish); Anita Kumari (crb); Atman (cb/Eggs); Kaiskynet (clb); Santusya (bc); Ulga (cb/Steak); Marazem (br/Chicken). 37 123RF.com: natika (tc/Ginger). Depositphotos Inc: serezniy (clb/Yogurt). Dreamstime.com: Artjazz (cra/cacao); Prostockstudio (bl); Ovydyborets (clb); Szemeno (tl); Margo555 (tl/Wheat); Anat Chantrakool (tc, cb); Nevinates (clb/Nuts, cla, crb); Voltan1 (cla/Plant); Gresei (ca); Donna Marie Vincent (cla/Oats); Iaroshenkomarina (cla/Pasta); Max Lashcheuski (cra/Noodles); Puripat Khummungkhoon (clb/Milk); Valentyn75 (cb/Oil); Oriori (bc/Jug). Getty Images / iStock: E+ / ma-k (tr); subodhsathe (crb/Rice). Shutterstock.com: Suradech Prapairat (cra). 38 Dreamstime.com: Photoeuphoria (clb); Mariusz Prusaczyk (cb); Aleh Varanishcha (bl); Staphy (bc); Teresa Virbickis (tr). Getty Images / iStock: Denis Lytiagin (cla). 39 Dreamstime.com: Elenatur (tl); Lacheev (tr); Simone Matteo Giuseppe Manzoni (bl). Getty Images / iStock: Photo Italia LLC (br). Getty Images: Stone / Timothy Allen (cr). 40 Alamy Stock Photo: aerial-photos.com (c). Dreamstime.com: Karen Appleyard (clb/Highlands); Neurobite (cl/coast); Minnystock (cr); Boris Panasyuk (clb); Artur Jakubowski (clb/Cave); Marcello Celli (crb); Iofoto (crb/Inlet); Fabio Lamanna (crb/Atoll); Denys Bilytskyi (clb/Lagoon); Pablo Caridad (br/Glacier); Biletskiy (br); Vogelsp (bc); Mrsixinthemix (bc/Stream); Marek Uliasz (bl); Wirestock (bl/Lake). Getty Images / iStock: Aekkarat Doungmaneerattana (clb/Bay); Anne Lindgren (cr/Canyon); frederikloewer (clb/Ocean). Getty Images: Moment / carlo alberto conti (cl). 41 Alamy Stock Photo: Dennis Frates (ca); Richard Green (br/Canyon); Ingo Oeland (br). Dreamstime.com: Chris Boswell (clb); Karsten Neglia (cl); Gleb Ivanov (tr); Maciej Czekajewski (cla); Premekm (cra); Vitaly Titov (bl). Getty Images / iStock: Fabian Gysel (cb). Getty Images: The Image Bank / James Warwick (crb/Nature). Shutterstock.com: Ely C (tl). 42 123RF.com: Vladimir Yudin / rrraven (tr). Dreamstime.com: Haizul (crb/Apartment); Macrovector (br). Shutterstock.com: Tupungato (cl/Housesx3). 43 123RF.com: Dimitar Marinov / oorka (ca). Dreamstime.com: Steve Allen (bl); Vicente Rubio (tc); Trondur (cla); Chris Hamilton / Chimpey (cla/Electricity); Cbechinie (cra/Cyclist); Timrobertsaerial (cl); Erix2005 (c); Valentina Moraru (cr); Mulderphoto (cr/Sewer); Olena Korol (cb); Peter Etchells (cb); Wing Ho Tsang (crb); Mineria6 (crb/Farm); Andreadonetti (bl/Statue); Physiodave (bc); Caoerlei (br/Wall); Jblackstock (br). Getty Images / iStock: bluejayphoto (cl/Bridge); Sean Pavone (tr/Dam). Getty Images: Westend61 (tl). Shutterstock.com: Anita van den Broek (tl/Port); Rita Image (cra); John_T (clb/Park). 44 Alamy Stock Photo: Christine Osborne Pictures (cla/pharaoh); Prawns (br); GRANGER - Historical Picture Archive (bc); Science History Images (bc/Compass); CPA Media Pte Ltd (cb/Empress); ICP / incamerastock (tr); Imaginechina Limited (clb). Dreamstime.com: Andreykuzmin (bl/Scroll); Tiago Lopes Fernandez (crb); Tanya Borozenets (cla); Edwardgerges (cr); Kateryna Kolesnyk (cra). Getty Images / iStock: Bjdlzx (bl). 45 Alamy Stock Photo: Vito Arcomano (cl); Lebrecht Music & Arts (bl); The Picture Art Collection (clb); Juergen Schonnop (tl); Erin Babnik (cla); FOST (cla/Empress). Bridgeman Images: © NPL - DeA Picture Library (cb). Dreamstime.com: Gillespaire (cla); Kvasay (br, crb); Therina Groenewald (cra). Shutterstock.com: Sanit Fuangnakhon (cl/Roman statue). 46 Alamy Stock Photo: Lebrecht Music & Arts (cla); North Wind Picture Archives (c); De Luan (cra). Dorling Kindersley: Egle Kazdailyte (crb). Dreamstime.com: Corners74 (bl); Kalman89 (br); Dreammediapeel (bc); Darren Curzon (cr). Shutterstock.com: Everett Collection (c). 47 Alamy Stock Photo: Everett Collection Inc / Ron Harvey (crb/Covered Frontier); Glasshouse Images / JT Vintage (clb); Montagu Images / Laurence Heyworth (clb/Sedan Chair); Pictorial Press Ltd (br, cl); PA Images (cla). Dreamstime.com: Abdellah Amed (cra/Smoke); Wisconsinart (br/High Wheel Bicycle); Simas2 (bl); Irinabal18 (bl/Electrobus); Hasan Zaidi (cr); Baloncici (cr/Clipper); Boarding1now (cla/Airplane); Bjrn Wylezich (cl/ferry). Getty Images: AFP / Patrick T. Fallon (tl). NASA: (cra, tc). Shutterstock.com: Arcansel (clb). 48 123RF.com: Piotr Adamowicz (clb); George Mdivanian (crb/TV). Dreamstime.com: Axstokes (cla); Monkey Business Images (br); Chernetskaya (bc); Kenishirotie (bl); Liouthe (ca). Shutterstock.com: GreenLandStudio (cla/Tablet); Dmytro_Kryzhanovskyi (cb); Third of november (clb); LuxMockup (clb). 49 Dreamstime.com: Axstokes (bl, crb); Prostockstudio (cra); Wavebreakmedia Ltd (clb); Rmarmion (clb/Library); Photographerlondon (crb/Field Trip); Meolia (bc). Shutterstock.com: NataliyaBack (clb). 51 123RF.com: Greek / Sergey Kolesov (bc). Dreamstime.com: Diego Vito Cervo (br); Ssstocker (b/X3); Scyther5 (br/Laptop); Chernetskaya (br/Singing); Nerss (cla). Getty Images / iStock: Bullet_Chained (tc); DragonFly (cla/Watermelon); spinspinspin (t/X5). 52 123RF.com: Smuay (cr). Alamy Stock Photo: Jessee Gorodenkov (bc). Dreamstime.com: Ekaterina Morozova (cl); Ventura69 (br). Getty Images: Corbis News / Horacio Villalobos (crb). Shutterstock.com: Muhammah Haseeb (clb); Pixel-Shot (bl); Wavebreakmedia (c). 53 Alamy Stock Photo: IMAGO / Peng Lijun / Xinhua / Joseph Mizere (ca); Douglas Scott (br/Food Server); PA Images / Anthony Devlin (clb); Peter Noyce GEN (tl); Keith Morris (tr). Depositphotos Inc: Gorodenkoff (cb); lucadp (tl/Smartwatch). Dreamstime.com: Allagreeg (bl/Robot); Sylvain Robin (cl); Dmitry Marchenko (cl/Car); Nikolay Antonov (cr); Info849943 (tr/Voice Assistant). Getty Images: Anadolu (cla). Getty Images / iStock: E+ / Olemedia (cra). Science Photo Library: Cordelia Molloy (bl). Shutterstock.com: Maryshot (cr/3D printer); Liu Yangjun (br); Fabio Oliveira 2020 (crb). 54 Dreamstime.com: Aaron Amat (cla); Monkey Business Images (cb); Richard Gunion (cra). Getty Images / iStock: E+ / Sturti (cla). Shutterstock.com: Naluwan (cla); ViDI Studio (cla/Solo). 55 Alamy Stock Photo: Travelshots.com / Peter Phipp (tr). Depositphotos Inc: Ahavelaar (tr/Drum kit). Dreamstime.com: Ababaka (cla/Violin); Wiseantwork (bl); Denys Kovtun (cb); Tarasenko Maksym (crb); Wave Break Media Ltd (cr); Xavier Gallego Morell (cra); Woraphon Banchobdi (cla); Prathan Nakdontree (tl); Rolmat (tl/Piano); Thomas Perkins (tc); Lunja87 (tr/Drums). Getty Images: The Image Bank / Peter Dazeley (clb). 56 Dreamstime.com: Volodymyr Melnyk (b). Getty Images: Photodisc / Sot (br). Shutterstock.com: Diignat (bl). 57 123RF.com: Konstantyn Kuznetsov (br). Alamy Stock Photo: Tetra Images / Chris Grill (tl/Victory); Visuals Stock (cl). Dreamstime.com: Convisum (tc); Steven Day (cr); Dmitriy Melnikov (bl). Shutterstock.com: Onur Ozgen (tr). 58 123RF.com: Spotpoint74 (cl). Alamy Stock Photo: Cultura Creative RF / Roberto Peri (cl). Dreamstime.com: Auris (b/Grass); Sandra Manske (bc); Sports Photos (clb); Denys Kuvaiev (clb/Pole vault); Michael Turner (crb); Leong Chee Onn (crb/Marathon); Serrnovik (cl/Baton Runs); MaxiSports (c); Darko Cvetanoski (cr). Getty Images / iStock: E+ / SolStock (bc/Discus); Nosyrevy (ca). Shutterstock.com: WoodysPhotos (cr/huddle). 59 Depositphotos Inc: PantherMediaSeller (cb). Dreamstime.com: Ammentorp (crb); Petesaloutos (crb/Artistic swimming); Renato Borlaza (clb); Aleksandr Makarenko (c); Sasha Samardzija (cra); Photosvit (cla); Michele Morrone (clb); Stoyo Petkov (tl); Zhukovsky (tr). Getty Images: AFP / Dirk Waem (cl). Getty Images / iStock: DigitalVision / Image Source (tl/still rings). Shutterstock.com: Alex Bogatyrev (tc); Hairul_Nizam (bl); Quintanilla (clb/Breaststroke); ID1974 (ca/Floor Exercise). 60 123RF.com: Jehsomwang (cr/Pirate hat). Depositphotos Inc: DenysKuvaiev (bl). Dreamstime.com: Creativesunday (crb); Monkey Business Images (bc); Panitan Kanchanwong (br); Mirela Schenk (cb). 61 Dreamstime.com: James Granger (br); Oksix (tr); Nagy-bagoly Ilona (cra); Dmitry Rogatnev (cla); Denis Pepin (cb); Sergeyoch (cb/Tennis Ball); Martin Mullen (bl). 62 Dreamstime.com: Chernetskaya (clb/lunchtime); Iftachul Farida (tr); Monkey Business Images (cla/registration, ca, bc, br); Wavebreakmedia Ltd (cra); Rido (cra/Break time, crb); Wiseantwork (cb); Konstantin Shishkin (cb); Anton Petrychenko (crb/school show). Getty Images / iStock: E+ / Lostinbids (bl). Shutterstock.com: Image Source Trading Ltd (clb). 63 Alamy Stock Photo: Justin Kase z12z (crb/Castle). Dreamstime.com: Digoarpi (tr/PALAMOS); Anna Tolipova (tr); Poznyakov (tl/Children); Iakov Filimonov (cla); Weedezign (ca); Monkey Business Images (cra, crb, bl, bl/secondary, bc, bc/colleges); Petr Zamecnik (cb); Seventyfourimages (cb); Hongqi Zhang (aka Michael Zhang) (br). Getty Images / iStock: E+ / Phynart Studio (tl); E+ / Pixdeluxe (tc); FatCamera (cla/Soccer). 64 Dreamstime.com: Prapass Wannapinij / Prapass (tr)

Cover images: Front: 123RF.com: belchonock cb/ (Gloves), lucyfry crb/ (Star), Rose-Marie Henriksson / rosemhenri cla; Dreamstime.com: Andreykuzmin bc, Axstokes clb/ (phone), MingWei Chan tl/ (Foot), Jose Manuel Gelpi Diaz tr, Elena Schweitzer / Egal cb, Geza Farkas bl/ (Bird), Gillespaire tc, Grafner bl/ (Ice cream), Hyrman tc/ (Carrots), Isselee crb, tl/ (Bird), Birgit Korber cb/ (Bunny), Konstantin Kirillov / Kvkirillov clb, Maglara bc/ (Jug), Nevinates clb/ (Blueberries), Photoeuphoria clb/ (Globe), Rimglow clb/ (Eggplant), Valpal crb/ (Pot), Guido Vrola br, Zhbampton clb/ (Beetle); Getty Images / iStock: Antagain clb/ (Butterfly), Bjdlzx bc/ (Calligraphy), Salmon Negro crb/ (Plates); NASA: tl; Back: 123RF.com: belchonock tr/ (Gloves), lucyfry cla/ (Star), Rose-Marie Henriksson / rosemhenri cla; Dreamstime.com: Andreykuzmin ca/ (Scroll), Axstokes clb/ (phone), Jose Manuel Gelpi Diaz crb, Geza Farkas ca, Gillespaire br/ (Gold), Grafner clb/ (Ice cream), Hyrman crb/ (carrots), Isselee tl, Birgit Korber tr, Konstantin Kirillov / Kvkirillov tl/ (Pan), Maglara cr, Nevinates br, Photoeuphoria tl/ (Globe), Rimglow tc/ (Eggplant), Valpal br/ (Pot), Guido Vrola cra; Getty Images / iStock: Antagain bc/ (Butterfly), Bjdlzx ca/ (Calligraphy); NASA: cl; Spine: Dreamstime.com: MingWei Chan b, Birgit Korber cb/ (Bunny), Photoeuphoria t; Getty Images / iStock: Antagain ca

All other images © Dorling Kindersley